Belligerence

NEW POEMS BY ANDREI CODRESCU

COFFEE HOUSE PRESS : : MINNEAPOLIS : : 1991

Cover illustration by Francesco Clemente.
Back cover photo by David Rinehart.

The publisher thanks the following organizations whose support helped make this book possible: The Bush Foundation; Minnesota State Arts Board; National Endowment for the Arts, a federal agency; Northwest Area Foundation; and Star Tribune/Cowles Media Company.

Many of the poems in this edition appeared previously in literary magazines and reviews. For a complete listing, see page 80.

Coffee House Press books are available to bookstores through our primary distributor, Consortium Book Sales & Distribution, 287 East Sixth St., Suite 365, St. Paul, Minnesota 55101. Our books are also available through all major library distributors, and through most small press distributors, including Bookpeople, Bookslinger, Inland, Pacific Pipeline, and Small Press Distribution. For personal orders, catalogs, or other information, write to:
COFFEE HOUSE PRESS
27 North Fourth St., Suite 400, Minneapolis, Minnesota 55401

Codrescu. Andrei, 1946-
Belligerence : new poems / by Andrei Codrescu.
p. cm.
ISBN 0-918273-85-4 : $8.95
I. Title.
PS3553.03B45 1991
811'.54 – DC20 91-14096
CIP

Contents

Belligerence

The Other End

Mnemogasoline

Outings

Belligerence

Belligerence

In the irruptive mode
I wear no hat
& hate what I see
in the rearview mirror
except silver balls.
When I was all the rage
I was in disruptive mode
& wore the instructions
on my Reeboks to a frazzle
between the lines of what
everybody read and the high-
way stripes painted there.
Actually shoes in those days
had no names but I was futurist.
Mealtimes at Hojo's & Wendy's
the plastic tablecloths
had squares in them and squares
in them and the prices were cheap
obsessively and people
in those days laughed
until their faces
became tic-tac-toe boards
& few could tell death to shut up.
Life was no fucking (pre)text.
Menus with everything under one
dollar were not unknown.
Anyway, only the greatest
could write it down. I was
among them. Since then, volcanoes
were miniaturized,
everyone gets to be
a little sick. I know
everyone who works here,
they are not happy.
I wear a dunce cap.

Circle Jerk

Nel mezzo del camino I found myself
in the middle class
looking at two diverging options:
ideology and addiction.
My triumph is to practice both.
Revirginate or Perish!
Learn how to read to trees!
(You never know who might be listening
when the class enemy is in the class.)
Can he be that hombre
who walk into town
followed by a slow caravan
of Toyota vans laden
with empty mail sacks
ready to BUY EVERYTHING?
The shelves, the things on them,
the stores themselves,
the clerks' personal effects,
watches, homes, mothers?
And gives them
whatever they ask for?
When this hombre leaves
the town wobbles like a great
plucked chicken
and shivers from cheap wind.
This hombre then sits
in on a card game
west of the Pecos
and tells this joke
to the members of the Cabinet:
An old Jew asks the Soviet
border guards for a globe
to see where he should go.
After hours of careful study
he returns it & asks:
Do you have another globe?

In the end we remember not the joke
nor the out-of-place place where
he tells it to the people
but the fact that we all detest living
through the adroit manipulations
of the small-print clauses
of our social contract.
Therefore you in the front row
wouldn't you rather
Do It Your Way?
Don Juan, narcissist
whose job is to upset order
and the authority spent
establishing it,
releases energy
teased into being
by his hat.
Once a man loses his taste for himself
he becomes completely unsavory: meat
spoils from within.
Others seep in through the chinks
and chomp chomp their way through heart & gut.
Two careless lovers are worth one thousand bankers.
The world is froth over the surface
of an untouched hard core
that first looks real,
then nostalgic, then Betamax.
I stagger from BBQue to BBQue
& never see sobriety anymore.

Seeing Out Of The Sub

for Alice

How do you see out of a sub?
I feel like I'm inside a sub, you say.
I feel like I'm inside a sub too.
The iron blimp in the Cabildo,
the confederate sub, possibly
the first sub consisting only
of a large iron body with a propeller
and a blind mariner inside her
hoping to ram a ship from underneath.
The mariner's hopes were the end of him.
Maybe it's best not to see out of a sub.
Maybe it's better to have a party.
Jonah's had rooms for millions.
The metaphor, I mean.
Maybe what we're inside of is a metaphor.
For the middle class, for instance.
The middle class is most like a sub:
Squeezed from below and squashed from above.
Despised by poets just like a shark or a sub.
I think what we need is a pun:
Remember the Chinese sub on the only
sleazy street left in Baton Rouge?
How we sought it out and delighted in its urban
cheapness? Its meat-filled blandness with lettuce
and the window where nobody sat?
That was a good place to look out of
because nobody cared what you were looking at.
The Chinese were busy eating their own product
when they weren't making more.
Our product, interest, and an interesting world,
comes about with looking like that
out of the window of a cheap sub shop.
The raw material is looking and looking.

It's no good being blind in a sub.
It's good watching from the sub shop.
The metaphor must yield to the pun.

Virgin Mule

The conversations of the French
Quarter mules in their stables
after a full day of pulling
tourists and voters over cobble-
stones is not espresso witty
and in their dark no TVs feed
them news of the ends of mules
elsewhere in the Middle East
and West. In our stables the ends
of others are a fact of atmosphere.
The yoyos on the mystery island
nextdoor are revving familiar tools
in backyard now gripped by failure
first of electricity than of
a meaner something that'll grow
into nothing we'll know in the A.M.
Once they were visitors like us
then they grew mulish in their
bubbles and pulled whatever
was put around their necks in-
cluding a banner that said, About
What Kills Us We Know Little.
On certain nights after a good
internal fight we hear the voice-
less others through the glass
fearfully sweet'n'soft like dough.
Oh let the monsters in. Help us
rise above our not seeing them,
may they let us into their eyes
as well. Banish the blindness
of these cobblestones, clop, clop.
But! Pffsst! Our notes are in-
complete. Loving you was
never on the agenda. Better
to sing as roughly as the stones.
On Memorial Day we had one

thousand hotdogs & counting.
Didn't visit a single graveyard.
We the Grant Wood folks scan
the sky for incoming missiles:
blips ourselves we understand
timing and touring in America.
The gilded dads in the portraits
sought the idealized continuity
now moving before us democratically
in showers of pixels and dots.
I'll go with the distracted mariner,
my lover, and we'll be in the world.
It will be late by then and dark.
We lyric virgin mules keep our
book of hours in a dream apart,
having stranded a billion turistas.
But we could not break the chummy hand.
Ready to brave the snow without a hat,
severe weather notwithstanding,
we merely nod and understand.

Telyric

Stand here, says the professional TV person.
She shields me from the sun with a silver shield.
The nuclear-trained soundman wires me to himself.
"Had top-secret clearance," he says,
"Shut four years inside a sewer pipe. Bad only
when the dope ran out."
"Top-hat clearance?" I ask.
"Our army's stoned and theirs is drunk."
A geezer stops: "He somebody famous?"
He spits in the fountain of the Immigration
& Naturalization Service said years ago
to have been an object of controversy
capable of shielding terrorists
in the goldfish rolls of its Dubuffet clusters.
The British cameraman who shoots me is proud
of his T-shirt from which a Scandinavian
plastic surgeon named Tord Skoog
rises blankly from humble beginnings
to an obituary in the *Scandinavian*
Journal of Plastic Surgery, and from there
unto thousands of T-shirts
from Patagonia to Maroc.
My telyric self bends in the sun-
solitude of its large puppethood.
A window of light is in the dugout roof
concealing the new national hero of Nicaragua,
pitcher Dennis Martinez.
I am connected with wires but not to sense.
The girl waves her white arm with the lamp:
I walk to her across the narrows
of my TV-less childhood.
Go on, put on the shield.
I throw the first pitch into the sun,
my tinfoil trembles like Skoog's fjord.

Leaves Of Nerves

Nylon is a wonderful thing in a city with trees.
Inside the wilderness of self
is outside but outside
is still inside
for Mr. Smith from St. Louis
who phones
to say all night I was inside
his head. "I was hoping
to speak to your message machine."
These are the very rich hours
of the Middle-Aged Duc of Poesy.
Onward & beyond
to the times when one would like
to write through
the machinery,
namely the love current,
but how much one belongs in the world
depends on how brightly
one talks to the police.
The aggression of health is badly understood.

The Introduction

After the interminable play
the beautiful actress
landed on him, a balsa plane
of starlight and dust
& asked to be presented
to the famous director.
All cities are Paris.
He effects an introduction
in a language no one
even pretends to understand,
Kurdish-Magyar, and night falls
about the yurts & colibas
as star & cast go off to the clubs.
He goes on & on explaining
why he is rooted to the spot,
an olive in the desert
but his listeners also
have their hands stuck
in front of them like branches,
olives too.
They are in fact a grove
where the philosopher walked
one noon. They have since then
imagined themselves right into
our century, in Paris.
What was at first chasm
became mountain then Chaos-town.
Theatre will never be the same
though the Japanese arrive in droves
to kill themselves beneath their shade

Demands Of Exile

for Dorin Tudoran

We are growing a bitter seed issue
of poets who can't go home again
in this here jar of a mag. Here are
squat men in fat suits papillon greasy
huddled in dark Chicago basements
perched on writing tables to leap
to Paris into Biedermeier inkstands.
Prettiness of course isn't the issue
when one has left behind all the pretty
things and is now at the mercy of scents,
happenstance, emigration, digestion.
Nor is the issue courage or top form
though both are necessary in order
to play sweep over the borders of official
form that need be completed and punctuated.
Not nostalgia not horror not righteousness
though in various degrees these are the alarm
clock perched on the wobbly armoire, child
of one Eternity and an enraged grownup
who saw Her bathing one day at the non-
political shore of childhood and caused
them to merge into a murderous
infinity whose issue is fiery death
and more death. For now they are kept apart
by the writing hand: the pen prevents
the closing of the fist and prices being
what they are it's a good thing too.
Not indignation intelligence rage
though in various bourgeois measure
these too once mixed well to steer
the hornet nest of culture causing bees
to rise from pamphlets into better print.
Home is a car on the road to a cottage
filled with storytelling mythmaking rustics

leaning on a future composed of woven pelts,
miles of sausages, milk and approximate figures
which form the antihistorical peak
where one rests in the company
of national fiction at its most formal ease
under a sky of homespun ambiguities and goat.
No those are not the issues though each line
makes the jar buzz and sets the fashion free.
The issue is ease, and when. The bitterness
thereof is the lack of it, the Sunday
afternoon going to bad movies
made by people one knows slightly,
then letting the haze of a cigarette
over Turkish coffee push the country
forward, a miraculous machine
that is the opposite of a cement truck.

Casino Pierre

The world goes on quite happily
without being pressured by anything more
than everybody in it.
Celebrate by ball-in-snow,
Aleut game played for fish.
But if it's Spring like now
baseball is best, for Cokes.
After watching for a year
I discerned where the ball was
thereby noting that after watching
for a while it's possible to see.
Playing with players
who spend their life playing
makes players play better
and all I need in order to be
a great player is to play
every day of my life
a program I have followed
religiously like a diet.
Ah, sun you are not a ball
but we just can't help using you that way,
like a baby and a vitamin.
Down the cautious streets
the circumspect century deflates.
Did the rest lose the war
of nerves or are they deeply
bored? Pumped full of holes
by wretched points of print & light.
Their watching is dull
and when they play it's
like rival offices banging
staplers on a square drawn on the floor
of the hall between them exactly
as the water fountain spouts blood.
Much peepee caca seriousness.
Shaving is both normal and welcome.

But there is only so much
of one's own stupidity
that makes sense or amuses
which is why the flesh is meant
and not the floor, or even the arena.
Everybody has to find out
what they were designed for
and though most voters never break
down the box with the secret
instructions, it behooves the great
bumbler to bow a humble head before
the waters we're close to drinking.
Being tolerant is the only revelation
I hope for. In America
everybody's in the electric
chair, the papers' low
voltage chair or TV's electric
high-chair. I never confuse
my inner life with my
secret one. Thus par example when I cross
myself on the street I don't
wink or say hello or tip
the iceberg in my heart toward
my hat. Fat is the body's
revolt against the rules.
Citizens, voting is not enough.
What hides in the already
enforced and geometrical
is neither safety nor bliss
but a nightmare needing time.
Optimism is the tendency
to underline. Vagueness
is any number of alien eggs.
One-liners are here to correct
your imperfectly understood idea
of what's possible. Spotlights
on the baroque flesh selling arks.
And aphorisms when they make the line,

know that only girls make it better.
They do it as if Spring was a given
which it is, in spite of the loud
summer in which the blinded wrap
their terror of the snapping bud
where I keep myself half
sleepy for the next call
from my Vantage Ultra Lights pack.

Roto: How The Bourgeoisie Dream

Human, step not into the Middle
    of the Road!
That's for Trucks!

*

I train the gaze.
Particularly useful center stage.

*

Not arrested *for* pot:
    arrested *by* it.

*

Earbulk.

*

The embarrassment of creation:
    I made *that?*
Certain days in December
the light surrounds me with the circumstances
of my birth.
I'm glad they made *this.*
    Prism jism.

*

All games are games of Yes and No.
The aggressor says Yes.

The defender says No.
Sweet fruits of victory:
    your enthusiastic subjects.
Bitter fruits:
    sore losers, ideological cases.

*

At the end of time
    au bout du temps
psi factors go through,
    cholera & ponies,
thud of great ideas:
    I had this advantage
in my mode of life.

*

A green bug
with a white border
on "the book that killed my summer."
I am what you might
call "a beneficial bug."
    I turned,
        walked away.
That butterfly had *legs!*

*

"Famous Places We Had Fights In Front Of"
    $8.95 in paper.
Where were you at those same times,
    O Bald Soprano?

*

Five years is not a long time
    to the steady heart.

*

Mmmmmmm. I want to
    be Taj Mahal!
        Mmmmmm. Candyman!
            It has been long.

*

Rising from the glib
    I become inchoate & inarticulate

thank God,
& then I shock myself with the truth.

The newspapers
flap around me
after replacing literature
but nothing flies.
Woman's body in the foreground
applies for historical site status:
was once battleground:
angels wanted in,
men wanted out,
but now it wants to be commemorated
but I think: Airport!
Certain Indians who live in books
are gathering
about the unaware reader.

He will be eaten in the bookstore.

Intention

for Tom Clark

Poems are be not intended
therefore I be always writin
never intendin

"Wake up/ have coffee/
write a poem/ what else/
is there?" (Elinor Nauen)

Wake up/ have coffee/ puzzle
dream/ about attention:
partial, full & deep./ Attention
paths/ are fascicles./ They work
negatively./ We engage only
inattention./ So go back/
to sleep/ dream some more/
about doors./ There is

the temptation to sprinkle
quotation marks about:
(and slashing 'em)
in that sense intention
abounds to make legit
the sense in which attention
could be intentional.

My intention is to make a poem
which includes all the great
lines ever written;

I intend this poem to be here
long after you've gone.

It was my intention to present
you with something
leading to sex. I intended

to apologize for the other night
with this humble poem
which has nothing to do with it.

I intend to sue you for character
defamation, let this poem serve
as a pre-subpoena. Intentionally,
I leave these little scratches
on your desk, I made them in a dream.

Intent upon my feelings I came
upon these words: I was full of good
intentions until I saw what I'd wrought
and swore to nevermore complain. Ill
intentions got me here with the ill
wind of the age filling the sails
of my poem: I'll make you something
on purpose to offset being lost.

It was the intention of all present
to palliate loss with literature:
it all came to naught when our leader
folded up the tent of his splendid
intentions, mounted anybody's steed,
took off in an uncertain direction.

What is found depends entirely
on being lost.

The failure of internationalism
is due in part to its containing
intention; likewise intonation,
internation, installation.

We knew exactly where to install
beauty but the electrical codes
are a century old, so we had
to start from scratch with noble

intentions but not much
enthusiasm which doomed us.

Furthermore, there is enough
intention in language
to sink any would-be orator
so why give headache to yousself,
who are a mess of botched intentions
as it is, Harry?

We considered the proposition
that the body might be
a superbly intentional
cooperative farmed out
to a cosmic purpose
and that the poem in its
organicity might be more
like the body than any-
thing less organized
and came to rest upon
the thought that the poem
like and as a body has no
choice, there being little
in nature or in art that
isn't organized instantly
upon expression: to make
is to order which is why
it is important to make
without a plan. Intention
lands one in bed with cliché,
which is somebody's old plan
to bed somebody else's old
plan – Don Juan's intentions

were from the beginning
to seduce the good ladies
of Seville though he had most
rudimentary ideas on how

to proceed, having only
an attitude and not a system.

Attitude differs from intention:
it is the Ur-ground of action
before the plan. Yes, I have
an attitude but it's no plan,
mother, I just want to set sail
for parts unknown, and later
when we recall the journey
for our homebound friends
we'll invent a whole new journey
we will never have unless we leave
right now, forget the telling.

I never intended to get around
the two things that smack of intention,
the two forbidden rocks upon whose flanks
many a traveler cracked and died:
post-intention and autograph.

Long after the journey's done
the post-intentional revisionist
plunges his Soviet pen into the facts
and spaces them intentionally
to make visible the line
on which flutter the bloody rags
of certain swollen egos.
I have done this, and I'm not proud.

Likewise the autograph by being
set before the journey like the word
journey before mounting,
pollutes the very journey with intention.
Of this I have been also guilty.

Forgive us our intentions, dear reader,
they were only attitudes gone flatter.

The Other End

The Other End

A CAVALIER OFFER

Would you like history?
Would you like history to begin with you?
We're right on target here at
the exact junction of present and future
round and perfect for the erection
of a wall after the destruction of the world.
The next word I say is the future.
You just say the word
when I say so after you say to
so it instantly becomes past.
The last word I said was the past.
Not all past is historical tho.
Not if it leaves no trace
of writing, buildings, film–
lotsa stuff for Mr. Clean.
Push my vacuum pedal.
Some traces are self-consciously
historical but
we won't let *that* stop us.
The Arc de Triomphe
built for a specific victory
projects into the future
on loan to marching boots forever.
The specific blesses
its perverse flow future to past.
Its "meaning."
Something to do with Napoleon,
a person better known in psychiatry.
A new tribe, the Wannabees
have been hitting the streets:
we all wanna be You!
A church means its connections
with the past architectural One
but tends to become grotesque
when it's resolved in art

which is another reason why, love,
I don't hesitate to snuff the past.
The meanings of traces are
food for sentimentality:
Hitler's boy architect, Speer,
made it to "look good in ruins."
It looked pretty good in four years.
You just give the word:
everything can look that good!
A four-year millennium is a commentary
but not a millennium.
The creation of fake history
without meaning from the start
is a business now,
an Arc to commemorate the nonexistent,
i.e., the future,
flowing backwards into
conjured delirium,
to empty into the hyped-up present.
They *waste* the future.
Our activities, amour, legitimize!

SUPPOSE THIS CAME TO PASS

It has.
In the East, history's remade.
In the West, erased.
On top of that
Big Words are coming back.
Ontology. Sport. Meaning. Millstone. Destiny. Deck.
The Debil. Der Gott. Life. File. Evolution. Mort.
Das Central Nervous System und Das Central Comitat.
Heavy-duty dudes *con* metashovels unearthing
Grand Clichés all ovah town
but mainly at the corner of Narcissus & Labyrinth,
a particularly, ugh, favorite psycho-intersection.
It's all this relativism, mahn,

bearing fruit & it ain't Fourier's pear.
Not mist, mysto-demagoguery.
Popular occult delusions
Speer-catch intellectual magma.
Another espresso please, easy on the *surfeit.*

NAMING SOME NAMES

One Gott-Debil runs this scene
goes by S.F.P.:
The Struggle for Power.
(So named by Andy
Schmookler, scholar without the tower)
Andy takes Old Testament Gott & makes him
natural science, turns pater into matter,
good & ebil into one thing,
like before theology–
In Golden Gate Park by Tripping Tree
during the time everybody got direct hits
of Heaven!
We were there getting a whole lot.
(Write here a history of the hat
around whose rim we walked
to mirror the theme.)
But it's a long way from the Gott-days.
S.F.P. resides outside
I mean inside
the text outside of criticism.
And that's all the outside there is.
Everybody's otherwise inside
learning to claustrophobe.
Every generality calls for a bigger one
but the beginning's shrouded in paradox.
The koan, the parable, the Sufi tale,
the Zen umbrella commission
the combatants. Where
does one come by tales like that

in the days of bits and bytes?
The operational model for utopia
is only handicapped by the words I use.
The ravages wrought by time sought
the inside of a cool tavern
to wrestle an Ouroborian beer snake,
infinite jaws, progressive traps,
horrible smoke, an incendiary jukebox.
Two more reasons he thought
why the Chosen People
write fundamentally upsetting books:
On the move they open to the
movement itself of ideas
since their raison d'être is a *promise*
they keep searching for the beginning,
re-establishing the ideatic chain
each and every time,
and they are ants on the vast body
of an Ocean-Text
all the romans-fleuves empty in.

THE SCHOLAR STORY

A gentleman scholar with a lit radish head
pulls up with all his earthly things
in the trunk of an old Volvo,
at a friend's who is not surprised
one evening in rainy November.
All his friends operate
the domestic machinery of time
just like the old car: sputter and die
on each others' doorsteps
and then go in for repair and stay
tho some are now sleeping under bridges
because it isn't always OK.
The Scholar has 1) Kaypro portable,
2) sleeping bag, 3) balls of deco socks,

4) fear of dogs (so Dog stays outside),
5) pedophobia (so hush the kids),
6) toothbrush,
7) special 20th-century genius that announces
its place among the structures is unique
& untenanted although it knows
only the inside of the atomic umbrella
where it doesn't feel safe,
and the human housing it, a short one.

The world is an institution. In it there are
divisions. Within those, sections. Report
anywhere. Everywhere is not home. Voice-controlled
left, image-controlled right. Drugs
to the middle. Use for leverage those
whose grandmothers wrote verse
for the Yiddish papers
last century—
bridges with one end up in the air:
the world they go to has vanished
but the other end is planted in these sons
whose persons read:
we cannot regret any longer
a world we cannot live in,
i.e., pre-WW2 Europe.
Not monster enough for huge gestures
but sufficiently in love with them
not to telephone.
We are waiting for the tone of the times to change.

Perhaps he isn't new but typical.
Intelligence, an appendix, residual,
or as in a book, useful,
self-endangered conspiracy,
solo center of toy-web,
dislikes women and children,
i.e., the powerless.
Tho he serenades them:

"I love the house I live in
with the creek running nearby
and the woman I live with.
Things are therefore good
especially with the trees
coming all out in flowers these days."
House, creek, woman, trees.
"But I can't work there
so here I creep."
The loner who goes crazy
if someone touches his car.
A new kind of guy, half-tech,
half-militant mason sent to set up
technofascist popcorn stands at the cross-
roads of Sentence & Reason.
We envy your ability to invent, he says.
Sure. And I'm the Pope.
Expressing regret for temporary
inability to control the poetic
sans products,
while looking no doubt
for some way to market it.

I immediately later change my mind.
He premeditates only the obvious.
I meet his mom
and his girlfriend Louisa-Marie.
There is tea, punch, petits fours, cake,
little sandwiches with the crust cut off,
and a fellow who plays the piano
even if you tell him to stop.
A Harvard PhD in nursing
recommends a feminist book on horses.
We are here to celebrate his book.
Everyone is friends of the good-natured nurse Louisa-Marie.
They take his entire stash of contributor's copies,
and only one of them asks him to sign it.
Everybody reads a line or two,
someone asks for a couple of words

explaining the thing.
He says,
“Skim it, you’ll get the idea.”
After that everyone goes onto the porch
to look at Union Memorial Hospital
looming ahead in many-windowed splendor,
and everyone says how much they like Baltimore.

“Can I interest you in a Hasidic story?”

It appears that a rebbe in rags
passes by a rich man’s house
and begs for a crust of bread.
The rich man sets his dogs on him.
A few years later,
the rebbe, grown wealthy,
passes by again, dressed in finery,
in a fine coach drawn by fat horses.
The rich man asks him in to be feasted.
When the soup comes,
the rebbe pours it on his clothes.
When the meat comes,
he takes it to the stables
and feeds it to his horses.
Why? the rich man asks.
When I came here before,
the rebbe says,
I was still the same man
but you didn’t feed me.
It is obvious that
you are not feeding the man
but the clothes
and the horses.

“Likewise, Harvard and I.”

The many-splendored windows of Union Memorial
are reflected in the proud face

no justification for l. endings — this is prose

of the nurse Louisa-Marie.
Behind them the sick converse with the beyond.

"The book is a revenge on father,
among other things.
I reinvent Evil as father,
then I kill him.
But I take no credit for it.
It came from elsewhere. It is
bigger than us."

The health PhD notes that the archers
on the cover are engaged
in a beautiful dance
though the dance is war.
By the Tree of Life
in Golden Gate Park–
"I saw beauty
in the universe
stretched about me
and containing me.
It was composed
of violent strife
of the rending
of flesh in history.
That was my Burning Bush,
does the Bible really say
that God didn't let Moses
into the Promised Land
because he broke the tablets,
or is that just speculation?"

The guy at the piano says it's in the Bible.
Moses,
another guy who
invented the father he set out to kill,
a more perfect father for the deed.

"I'll see to it that
the last humanist haha

is gone by dawn.
We create nothing:
S.F.P. makes certain
expressions & their by-products
inevitable.
I trace the demise thus:
Galileo shoves us out of the center of the universe.
Darwin out of the center of nature's world.
Freud out of fate's pilot seat.
Me, out of history.
Individual choice is the very thing
that takes *general* choice from us.
Individual choices create anarchy
and anarchy is ruled by S.F.P.
which infects the whole
with its imperatives."

It all comes down I say,
to another
deification of power,
a popular thing these days.

The scholar takes off his shoes.

"Opposition, if you're thinking it,
is only possible through the creation
of *reasonable systems.*"

Fascism by any other name.
I mean, how much power
do you use to restrain power?
How do I get outside?
The world's been shrinking too much as it is.
They're taking down the outside as we speak.
The penis, a tough survivalist, alone holds the fort.
The soul wants to get out of the rain
like any pitiful bourgeois.
The proverbial They becomes It.
It is bigger than us and indifferent to us.

It pursues only its own aims
& the little in us that isn't It,
our so-called humanity is lost.

Never say
it says
it speaks
it talks
because it
does not

Of the whole grace
it can express only the part
that understands its own impotence.
To describe the working
of the outside in this here ah lingo
is to destroy il paradiso by the motion.
Oh thing where hast thou gone?
Language unweaves the world
it weaves when we give the spiel.
Without its gates of Jews,
il Paradiso stands unmoved
inside the humid critters
taking out the garbage only
to find themselves immersed
in the starbright riches of the azure flowing sea
where all at once everything that is *not you*
is THERE!
And then to get in a slow biz like this!

Only the garbage didn't get taken out.
It's still there,
it's too dark outside, hon.
We likes it in here
under the atomic umbrella
even as Something pushes us out,
we can do it tomorrow.
So we lie and lie ourselves open
to the devastation of divine indifference

—a redundancy—only to end up
reinventing morality,
the science of indoor living.

Which brings up a Question:
did God *really* give Moses the tablets?
Or did Moses carve them up there,
with a primitive tool,
knowing that the Burning Bush
didn't really give a damn—
being neither Good nor Bad
nor Concerned—
but that if he wanted his people to survive
he had better come up with something quick.
And when he did
God the Bush *did* get pissed off
and fixed it so that Moses
would never get home.
Does *anything* give a damn?

"S.F.P. gives a damn
about what serves It.
It is not served by morality.
Moses invented an aberration:
he rose against S.F.P.
Morality is a system of natural value.
Natural value is based on biological selection.
What is selected is good
because it is what works.
The body is good
because it is the best nature has
come up with.
We must defend
the integrity
of our organism
by means of morality.
But in Civilization
we confuse
the aims of

Power
with the aims of our integrity.
But the two differ.
In the undifferentiated,
amoral primal It
we had no choice.
But in Civilization
we do not share nature's purpose,
so we must split It consciously
into good It and bad It.
We have to invent
a conscious Manichaeism
on the basis of what's good
for us.
But since too often what is good
for us
is not good
for the rest of this world,
which has in it also birds
and trees and seabeds,
we must apply morality both inward
as a kind of brake
and as a weapon against
the objective power of It.
We have to perform
the same operation as Moses:
transform
divine indifference
into benevolence."
But the Good we bend to our purposes
is weakened,
while the Bad grows stronger.
(It's the only game in town.)
So Moses helps us along
the path to destruction.
Realizing this, he committed suicide.
It wasn't God
kept him out of Paradise:
Moses didn't want to go there

because he knew
it was a made-up place.
Moses didn't want
to see his metaphor
come to life,
didn't want to live in his
invention. He had rent asunder
the sacred energy,
just as we split the atom.
He must have thought that by refusing
to authorize his fiction
he could put divinity back together.
His suicide was an attempt
at synthesis
by removing the author
from the work.
Too late.
The split atoms don't unsplit.
Differentiation is evolution.
The demiurgic is destructive:
the universe it creates
destroys the universe it describes.
The word is chemical.
Reason and Poesy.
Containment and Escape.

FRANCHISING THE FIGHT

The only way to fight
is to open up franchises
hoping that the thing
released somehow
from centrality
includes but does not limit
the body it defends.
Reason,
humanity's collective building,

perhaps the edifice
of culture itself,
isn't very old
and is rather puny
when inspired babble rises.
Revelation
and prophecy
unreasonable speech,
synergistic and viable
disintegrates the sacred It
deconstructs itself
obliquely even as it follows
an almost mathematical morality.
A "scientific" poetics
and a "poetic" law.
"Mechanization" and "objectification"
are fully present
in the language of the lamentations.
Fighting common sense
one arrives in the City of God.
This fight causes the Debil-God to come.
Debil looks like an assistant professor.
The text has certain therapeutic effects.
The thinking that it encourages is palliative.
It is tonic and absorbing and keeps us awake.
It makes staying up a pleasure.
The indifference
of power accounts
for the failure of generation
after generation
to bring about peace.
We feel most utopian
and least articulate
under the umbrellas
made from Ebil itself.
Words are only tenuously
connected with sense.
We cultivate this tenousness
as if it were the whole territory.

The tragicomedy of utterance
is that we all trample
the same narrow isthmus
between *word* and *world.*
The L in the belly of the word
is the Khyber Pass,
the center
of ambition.
Its conquerors control
the back and forth.
The power now controlling
the traffic between
reality and symbols
is journalism.
When poetry was in charge we
saw more reality, more world.
Now we see more symbols, more
words. Some of us stand
in the middle of the traffic
screaming: THERE IS NO BRIDGE!
(And in the Bay Area too!)
The bridge groans, barely capable
of handling the weight.
(The Trampled Isthmus)
The bridge is a body,
an Exquisite Corpse
formed by the former guard
who cannot die.
By offering the golemic corpse
of a literary corpse instead,
they hope to separate
literature from physiology.
The inability to separate them is
what we die from.
When their Exquisite Corpse dies,
the gods will
take the bridge with them the way
they would have taken all of us
if we hadn't made them this.

What's more, they will enjoy
it better: less of a mess.
We interpose
a memorable body between
their murderous desires
and their sentimentality.
Graffiti on the bridge:
Hormones + Experience = Reality.
Even so, downhome narration
rarely fails thought,
tho thorgasm eludes our poets.
We've got to hit us with the Tertium Organum.
It is our good fortune to possess
the key to inspiration
in yonder cabinet
and our misfortune to be forced
to intention. Fortunately
our intentions are (not) good. Had
they been (not) bad we'd be tense.
We sit on the cyclone
fence, dangle feet over the gene-
rators below. Sitting on the fence
used to be a simple affair. A country
sort of thing with a straw twixt
teeth. Anxiety's industrial now.
Nero's neon, had he had it,
would have been hard-core. At
the core of his madness lay neon.
All bright future things lie
at the upset cores of the insane.
The upset cores of the insane
are generators. Their humming
turns the engine of history.
Our sweet predilections and love
connections feed it juice.
Our shells feed it oil. When it gets
enough intention
it runs smooth. But when a core lights
up without the yoke of sense

it trembles, sputters, chokes.
Ah, misery inspired by pure rant!
We equate adventure
with violence, mistaking the
the jukebox cores of the insane
with the ordering of goats and sheep
on a statistical hillside.
Reason is bricks, we said,
on them we build the reasonable
edifice of science.
We eat the use.
The poet on the other hand waves
doubting hand in dead air,
sunbathes on the roof or, worse, jumps.
The engine of history does not
hide in the brick edifice of science.
Nor does the house of bricks hide
inside the engine. Nor is
the house the engine or vice
versa. When faced with in-
compatible metaphors science
calls poesy on the race phone:
cortex to cortex.
I will not help you, says poesy,
until you get these bricks out of the way.
I can't see the sky.
So philosophy clears les débris.
And this engine, poesy says, hums too loud,
it disturbs my reverie.
Science shuts off the engine
with a communist potion from his kit.
Great silence falls between the metaphors.
The sky is a perfect picture of the past.
The silence the perfect future.
In the present tense we the tense
wait for something to say itself.
Philosophy holds its vial frozen
at the exact moment of its use. Nothing
budges. The universe is present. An insane

core lights up. The engine coughs, it
starts, it sputters. The dinosaurs come
out of the books. The mechanic, a Mr.
Nietzsche, wipes his forehead with a greasy
rag. A Monsieur Pasteur
vows that the engine will not move. He
hastily begins to pile bricks in front
of it. NO PASARÁN! he shouts. A wall
of reason stands before the thief
and his demented motor! The unexpected
and the shady have done the job.
Eternally the honest sucker is thwarted
by the cunning of these two. Eternally
he vows to set things straight. Next
time he's taken worse. And always
there is more blood on the floor and more
psychology. The bricks are books,
the tower has a million floors.
It falls inevitably down
between irreconcilable metaphors.

Meanwhile at the party
merely a rose away
Union Memorial in the Exxon-lit night
was still–
we could hear the flowing of the River Styx
sighing under the wordrain that beats on it.
Afraid of nothing but leeches
we couldn't practice what it preaches.

Three days later Scholar left for the creek,
the woman & the flowering bougainvillea
leaving behind only his word-mantilla.
The anxious telephone burst several times:
"Is my book merely a book?"
It's as great as *The Origin of Species,*
his friend said.
To himself: A book is a book.

Mnemogasoline

Mnemogasoline

Under the tropical moon
the peaceful hooker
discoursed on the Gestalt God
with a cat on her shoulder
slowing the motorists down.
She was without fear
as the small Honda went past
bound for the warfront against auto-amnesia
being waged on the old narrative line of defense.
The Honda stopped and a technical
designer at Disney Studios,
who that very day
had been observed doodling on the job
a thing unrelated to Mickey,
and accused of spying,
got out and advanced toward her.
Rather than apologizing, I quit,
he to her explained.
Go to sleep,
said the peaceful hooker.
She wore white stretch pants
& a red sweatshirt inscribed OPIUM
& she took his hand and laid him
on the steps at Sproul Plaza in Berkeley.
He woke up surrounded by a forest of sleeping bags.
A protest was being held, concerning Apartheid.
It was just before dawn.
The rows of moonlit bodies looked like plaster
tempura dishes in the windows of Chez Japan.
The intimate tempura of sleep hid the sushi of youth
& filled the present with the romance of another time,
but inflated slightly like a Hong Kong import.
A lightly spun idea dew plied lightly the multicolored polyester,
leaving a dark trench where the speed of commodification
met the definition of symbolic exchange values,
i.e., the labels were inside out,

overturned by nocturnism.
The technical designer stretched in the last ditch of his youth
& rose to embrace the bagels wafting from the bistros.

On the street that morning at about 8:20 AM
an ancient man with Pomo d'Oro hair and a sharp
Mephistophelian moustache
was making a telephone call
from a heavily graffitied booth that had
miraculously preserved a clean Southern pane.
He was calling somewhere very far because his lips
formed a small sorrowful noose
like an egg smashed in at the top by a child during
some ancient Easter, soon to be tossed, child and egg,
into the chute of history whence little returns.
I recognized him: it was the lover
of the last Queen of Romania,
a famous playboy of another era.
When I looked, the ancient lover's face cracked:
I saw apologies sucked out of various moonlights
in countries no longer on the map
& he appeared to say, or rather his face did:
"I didn't sleep with her. Very sorry."
But the pomade in his hair said otherwise.

I opened the door of the cafe
for the belle holding five iced coffees,
who said: "You read my mind."
"It was writ large," I spoke,
"but I'd like to read your body better."
My speech went unnoticed,
having never truly left my throat until this very moment,
but the ancient playboy behind the wall of graffiti
put his hand over his heart and keeled over,
a vessel of Eros sunk by a phone.
I was the first on the scene
& was reluctant to use the very phone that he . . .
but I did

& paramedics entered the scene in spattered angel suits.
Unbeknownst to anyone I gave him the lover's salute,
silently before the medics came.

In our mutual country several thousand miles to the east
the mad dictator Ceauçescu, a triple-chinned gargoyle,
whose place in Hell is being kept by toothless political
prisoners fanning the flames with tracts
(he had once succeeded the man who'd overthrown
the queen the dead man loved)
was ordering the demolition of the ancient capital
to make room for statues of himself.
A 16th-century church gave way to a badly executed bronze head.

I notice that the etiquette of gazing in America's cities
has to do with loss of concentration due to zoning.
The absence or the presence of cafes
is proportioned in direct ratio to gazing eyes.
What looks oblique is really lost
opportunities in real estate.
Other places employ other gazes, terrain-modulated to take in
adventure.

Even the old are only myopically casual:
they too are working for love.
I am tortured by certain looks
I get in dreams from people in my past
who, not content to die and tear a hole in me,
continue staring from beyond.
I find a nervous tropical translation
of those looks in humid cities like New Orleans
or Rio de Janeiro.
In these the dark is moist.
The buildings I would build from the crossings of gazes
by the dead with the living
stand in my mind, blue lines in a blueprint on the immense
glasstop table of a Texas developer.
I would replace the dictator's statues with those.

Besides standing, sheltering, and allowing one to be observed
while seemingly unaware, by one or many,
or to be invisible if one wished,
these buildings would change every hour,
a mix of Persian gardens, Paris cafes, Casbah tents,
Marseille alleys, movable streets, floating flowerbeds,
swaying awnings, and dark dives where to wallow
in the sadness of running out of things to buy.
The passive-poetic of night-day reversal
will enhance the mode of sexy difficulty.
I hope to instill in the construct a feeling
of phones ringing in the steam, and clothes falling
around an ontologically attractive metaphysical node set into the
structure at all levels to make it possible to turn anywhere
one feels the benevolent divine urge of the subject.
What is a subject?
Something that can hold, I expect, for many pages, hours, miles.
Why are your moods so *long?* someone asked me once.
At the time I barely knew the joys
of the heavenly fifth wind,
where you stand straining the membrane
on the back of all things
against the current of time.
But now when I go into the unknown
I like to travel a few miles.
Everywhere is a new city, everything must be seen at once.
There are, of course, *moments,* peaks where
one story is soldered to the next,
narrative ditches where flattened against the seams
the old demons crouch waiting for sentiment to let them out.

After I left the scene of the death of the lover from the Old World
I took the Greyhound bus to Baton Rouge.
A cowboy was telling a girl about his dog Skipper
how many times she ran away before she made it
& about the time he was a welder on board a ship
& a dog kept him prisoner all night one night in Panama,
with a black man who told him about another dog

who jumped after someone who went down in a pond somewhere
in a southern region of the United States known as Dogtown, AL,
& she remembers the day her daddy shot her dog
for biting the village doc whose own dog then took a ear off
Chunky, her own mutt—and the bus didn't rock to a stop,
it growled into the nine-dog night
describing a circle that took in the welder, me, the bus,
the years, the blueprints of desire, all surrounded
by a thick circle of dogs.
Don't forget, the former ship welder said,
about the girl killed last night in this morning's newspaper
by a mad dog, "prob'ly a nigger or a kike or sumpthin."
"It don't take much for a kid to disappear,"
says the tattooed girl,
a real history of American bad girlhood on her,
blue arrows through red hearts of link chain.
America's wretched riders are arranged by subject matter.
"Dog." "Tattoo." "TV Guide."
There are no foreign students holding Ameripasses.
The front half of the Dawg packs bibles and guns.
The back half is escapees from institutions,
free-lance murderers, sexual desperadoes,
swamp flowers of genetic damage.
"I left a bible in a motel in Hollywood,
and now they are making a movie from the parts I underlined,"
my bench mate tells me.
I study the tattoos in front of me.
The pictographs testify to the narrative urge.

Later that month in the avantgarde capital of San Francisco
another movie is being shown.
It is black and white.
Many frames tremble. A girl in one of them opens
a chill window, letting in the fog.
In many frames thereafter she opens the window.
There are also upside-down parts in a park.
The girl's knee decked in a deco sock.
A door frame.

The filmmaker explains that he has a birth defect
& that this film essay on love
is proof of a dyslexia from which fountainlike
a plethora of bad decisions have dogged him all his life
until they issued upon the weary frames.
Having committed also lifetimes of them before this life
he sees the sign of healing upon himself in the movement
of the handheld camera, helping him to switch
polarities, so that he might become
that glory of late research, a Left Hander, a South Paw.
To this end, and to hasten its coming,
he does everything with his left,
leaving trails of calligraphed paper
in a childish left hand behind him
in cafes and cinematheques.

I have a mild dyslexia as well.
An inability to distinguish left from right.
I call it organic anarchism.
It saves time.
But the filmmaker always going left
needs constant readjustment, as he can feel megadoses of vitamins
traveling him like beatniks through the world's *inclinations*
which must be *corrected* by utopia or eternal life,
whichever comes first.
His body is defective, he believes, in places
where it is unfocused on by moral chemistry,
just as reality's defective where the shaky lens is shut.
We, organic anarchists, *au contraire,*
see reality's defects precisely in those places
where art's been stepping in and making scenes.
My hometowns, all of them, are sadly now
overrun by artists who are the churchkeys letting
the tourists out of the sardine cans of the middle class.
Reality's birth defects are magnified by art
until tourists with opera glasses stand
in the pretend infant urine of false representation
looking out into the fake past,

rendered useful to the connoisseur, alas, but lost
to all native sense until retired into a single postcard.
My own childhood town, transformed by reference,
gathers its platonic blueprints into a ball
& rolls into view, there to become a drop containing
a time of pristine transport,
while being, as far as I can tell,
a postcard in the hand of the baffled
tourist who pays dearly for his holograms.
The fake town is redesigned to show even the wear of adoration,
even the places where memory works it over,
tear grooves, canals polished by tongues,
long unsplintered beds dug by stretched index fingers
into the angels pointing at the ceiling of Teutsch Cathedral,
a veritable army of stretched hands and arms.
It would be good
if the shoddy translation job in inferior materials
could stand in contrast to the shining drop in my sometime head.
It's unbelievable how shabby the real Rome is!
Like kept prisoner by a dog on board the working history of the world.
Poetry plies the rift like a bird dog in a Mannerist painting.

"Is Mr. Wisdom here?"
"No but mebbe I can find Mr. Stupid for you."
"I am very very sorry to have disturbed you."
"You didn't disturb me. You fucked with my mental *balance!*"

The appropriateness of the locus
of the crime, i.e., "the breaking of the shoe."

Seeing the back of a beautiful girl walking,
I can feel her with my whole body. Amazing.
I must prevent her from turning. It becomes my job.
Maybe she's not a girl at all, but a mailbox, or a newsstand.
Walking behind her downTelegraph Avenue, this lovely Sunday morn,
I wonder if sex is the opposite of schizo-
phrenia.
Finding myself philosophizing behind her

easy-swinging lovely back, I think to overcome her
and to ask, "Is sex the opposite of schizo-
phrenia?" –
when she turns around,
& smiles at me directly slicing me in half:
"How are you this gorgeous day?"
"Yourself ?" I say astonished and inaudible,
meaning her Self as different from her back
which I somehow feel "I know," that it is "mine."
"Oh fine," she says, meaning her back too.
She touches the red frame of my glasses:
"It feels good," she says,
"to take a break from the Eros seminar."

Electromagnetic field reader & manipulator
just inside the gates of my head, shakes his head.
Ah yes the fields exist and they are knowable.
There is nothing bigger than them: not even Time.
But there's a rub: Timing.
I'm on my way to the airport and she's one day late.
The timing of knowledge is thc crux.
But in her crux time is made right.
The crux is always present to the crucial.
Mistimed knowledge lines the pits
the true originals lie in becoming drops.
But there was never a time when things could have been different.
They are always different.
Does uselessness invalidate seeing?
Should schizos be protected like brujos or restored like vases?
In the sexualized field, analysis (chemistry) encounters action (faith)
for purposes of reassessing the description.
The tearing of the veils,
the breaking of the crust,
are immediately followed by the blinding
revelation of organic
complexity underneath.
To make another whole it is necessary to remake all the parts.
Which are themselves wholes formed of further particulars.

There is no self-generated
return to the surface
because there is no "self."
The fragmented cluster of particulars
in a state of rapid disintegration
whirls by in search of a matching cluster
& is further pulled apart.
Violence from the outside has certain advantages
if the object to be put
back together
serves some function in that state.
Should I now fall apart.
I am doubtful if enough
usefulness could be found in me –
barring discovery of the drops –
to justify
bringing me back to one unit.
Better to mark each part with the word *Taboo.*
But if you're sexy enough they'll name a perfume after you.

At the truck stop where America's last free storks nest,
a killer leaves a Popeye's chicken box.
Inside it is the hand of formerly his best friend.
The former welder on the bus retches and smokes dust.
The ship's cook once made nail clipping soup.
For one hundred bucks Greyhound is good forever.
"We haven't been off the bus for eight years,
except to buy Popeye's." Sunsets, sunrises,
nausea-lined faces form solidly into a coffin bashing
rudderless against the TV.
We on the other side let's wave at the lumpenproletariat.
Sooner will sulfates cyanide silicon selenium salt
go through the eye than minor psychos into America.
Who remembers Juan Corona?
Gacy?
Whitman of Texas?
Ng and the Chowchilla boys?
Where is the handsome Black Doodler

with his sketches of soon-to-die lovers?
The Zodiac Killer who scratched his stars on corpses?
Charles Manson of the Beatle-mysteriumed Bacchae?
Williams of Atlanta, bridges, strangled children, night?
Where are the newspapers of yore?
The ship of gore?
Scuzz, scum, flotsam, dusted, juiced, sick,
the Dark goes Greyhound and Big Red, and hitches
toward the TV glass.
Wave harder now.
There used to be a way through the glass,
some of the old-timers remember.
You could hitch a ride through literachoor.
Why, there was Kerouac.
You could go through him right up to America
& it was like you'd always been there.
Well, half in and half outta da glass at least.
There useta be a mesh of coincidence right about here,
& conjecture, riding the narrative folds to some under-
standing of Eros in liberty, and then it was a short hike
home.
I'm looking, but for what?
It's been mended.
There is a preacher in the hole collecting a junk army:

Hallelujah brothers & Hosanna!
It was a dark hour when they put him in the grave.
It was Friday!
But Sunday is here!
They don't celebrate Easter in Poland today like we do
They have the jackboot on their neck!
It's Friday in Poland!
But Sunday is coming!
The Soviets are strafing villages in Afghanistan
Killing women & children
It's Friday in Afghanistan!
But Sunday is coming!
And Napoleon was broken at Waterloo

Where he kept hitting and hitting
But Wellington's line wouldn't break!
Two thousand years ago Satan threw everything he had at Jesus
But the rock didn't break!
And today godless Communism throws everything against
the rock of faith & the rock doesn't break!
And the media knows not an iota of the Gospels!
One day is coming when you'll turn on your TV & only the voice
of the Gospels be coming through!
It's Friday in the world
But Sunday is Coming!

The drama of Eros and Self goes on in the pews
where the cross-eyed folk wink at each other.

Back in Berkeley, California, I am given a starring role
In the Opéra Bouffe of Exile!
A million forgotten ideas fight for my ear.
I sing the part of the Ear.
My fellow wanderers want my ear.
No, no, I say, what you want is America's Eye!
But they are all stubborn like my mother.
"Since she became a cyclops, we had no rest, your mother and I . . ."
There are ministers without portfolios singeing their barbered
whiskers on a violence without victims . . .
Academics without chairs, desks, carrels, universities . . .
Monarchists without a king tripping on the red carpet of the
hotel lobby with vials of blood in their palsied pockets
from which they furtively sip as their wrinkles briefly
disappear . . .
Fascists without leaders, fuehrerless fanatics . . .
Nudists dressed in the armor of discarded truths . . .
Icon painters falling to their knees with heavy wooden crosses
about their meaty necks . . .
The very lover of Queen Marie who has reappeared with his plasterboard
hair wandering all over the map of our vanished country,
carving new valleys of Vitalis broadcasting yellowed
instructions and codes carrying from phone booth to phone

booth that sickle-thin fin-de-siècle smile
that says always, forever, I didn't really, besides
it wasn't any good, it was a literary idea, she was
a writer you know . . .
but no book will ever be about us?
I see ideologues of splinters of splinters
arranged in tiers, a political cake of parties
on frayed tablecloths in unrestored European hotels
waiting for the beringed fingers of a native autocracy
to plunge through the icing for a taste of their hearts.
Arranged arachnid-style around the chandeliers
are painters of icons "in the traditional manner"
waiting for a signal to descend upon the cake flames
which are tall Orthodox silver crosses
shaking aromatic powder or the dust of the IXth Arrondissement.
They have traveled long distances to praise God,
& have some cake, have some cake.
God is everywhere an occasion for a gâteau-da-fé.
But perhaps they all wait for muscle, not for religion.
For young punks to back up the bitter yeast of their spectacular
escapes from everywhere into the story
no one wants to hear, alas. Like tremulous
and not-so-young mademoiselles from another century,
refined beyond present-day understanding,
they speak 25 languages & not one of them the vulgate.
The hotel's tarnished gilded salon trembles during the verse-recitation
of the boring epic,
wishing it was listening to Charles Baudelaire instead.
Everything désuet & lost is in the dusty escritoires,
shorted violetas, misclustered chandeliers.
I meet a young woman here. In the shade of her violent eye makeup
are her recent memories when with 13 of her friends
she lay in front of the President's limousine,
her hi-heeled shoes pointing an ultimatum at the spiky
tyrant in his Brooks Brothers blazer & Kalvin Klein jeans,
as her high-placed family trembled awaiting the phonecall
from the secret police.
In my day a certain gentleness still attached to the electrodes,

a multithreaded rag of innuendos especially licensed
by one's lycée to pass themselves off as metaphors.
Brutality hadn't quite become art for art's sake.
I meet a great critic.
After 5 years in prison,
he is only interested in California boys.
They say, he tells me, that this is the capital
of perverted sex! I am a FEROCIOUS pervert!
They have diseases here,
an alarmed dissident folklorist tells him.
They might catch something from *me,* shouts the critic,
& the pathos of lost diseases shines briefly
in cot B of his former cell,
political, historical, intellectual diseases that flare
in his joints and at the seams of the world's wounds giving
the critic's eyes a certain flaming luster.
What is a virus to those?
Places where folk die of philosophy
don't share geography with places where people die of diseases.
They share no air, no words, no maps.
Three to a room, they're kept
waiting for people to enter & tear
apart in interesting patterns.
I am conversing with the chief ex-spook from America's
Secret Radio Police who is about to break the news
to me that I make a lousy Ear
when the lobby fills suddenly with humans in wheelchairs,
torsos on skateboards,
arms in slings,
steel hooks,
bandanas over deep body holes.
The chief says, "Here is the next convention,
they booked them one day early, there will be a mess."
Exile has its internal tourist attractions and a timetable out of whack.
Mistimed etc lines the pits etc.
I watch my countrymen carrying an unfair argument with the ghosts
trapped in their memory drops, and I wish
I could rain on them to take them home.

The old country and their youth are intact in the blue atmosphere
around each and every one of them,
& they are ready to die for it.
Some would do double duty and also die for art.
I stand astonished at the certainty of what art.
A bouquet of little indulgences waits crammed in the jewel box
of my memory to be pried ajar by my fellow exiles.
I enter the escritoire of meta-finances, filled to the transoms
with hotel bills and laundry tickets,
& look at the many cities below
unchanged in the geography of desire:
Vienna, Buenos Aires, Tangiers, Paris, London, New York and Caracas.
They are my mantilla's arousal, my calling card,
this premier assent of cities of exile into the heart
of my explicative genius at its flood-season height.
A drop would suffice to render understanding unto all
but the operation is not visual, not designed for a flat Eros,
though it is a little shabby
like Spain maybe before the Conquest.
What can't be had is worth equipping an armada for.
What is invisible always has a door.
A solid brass door encrusted hopefully with the eyes of romance.
It's Berkeley, Brazil, Lima, Bangkok, or France.
The esprit of despair takes poets by the throat to produce
not a Classical Age but a holding pattern, a sterling fork
to tune the streets for better holding forth.
I am breathing through one hundred straws,
each one designed to suck in another *paysage*
& I am bleeding through eight hundred little wounds
each one mined by an expatriate's *vernissage*
which is why when they hold me a certain angle like an ear,
in the sun, I am a copper sieve sifting red flour on
piles of little uncirculated shiny coins labeled *Mnemogasoline Drops*.
Royalties on the books that result thereof are paid by the wind,
alone among the elements to read.
The whirring of irridescent scholarly beetles bores the light.
I did set out to be an icon, it's true.
The people in my village wished fervently for it,

even though I was born in a rather large city,
& always had the lowest opinion of hicks – even when,
I shamefully confess, the Lord lowered his rifle on the peasants
& had them made first into dust, then into symbols.
I became a sort of icon I called The Sword and the Mascara.
There are no watchers, of course, and this is good.
It would be fine if there were watchers who knew that the watched
were hiding something even if it was only their artificiality
which made them act that way.
Which way is that?

The victims of art are now simply called citizens.
They display their victimization
like a passport to civilization.
Their formal bodies are art. I mean, mine is.
We stand between the books and cannot be told apart.
If we are picked up we open everywhere and can be read quickly.
We stand in galleries mournfully unable to look as modern as that.
We walk out of the pages of books and back on the streets
lined with epochal reminder craft just like the entries we mean
to stay in when our bodies go.
We are enticing but there aren't any observers.
Who can stand outside to say Ah?

The problem with autobiography
is that you find yourself in places already written up.
The world takes on an insufferable literary air.
Everybody's in it & they are always home.
There is a volume of déjà vu.
Even if you have changed things ever so slightly.
The déjà vu is distorted ever so literally,
reality takes on that defective air,
a defect of translation passing for a defect of birth.
The shadows of the defective turn on their hinges,
tarnished by reference to adoration & translation.
Say what? Say what? Repetition is not exact?
Hence realism's impossible?

The world believes in sex, the absurd and gymnastics,
& I *could* to keep it at that,
but even with my back to the beautiful girl I can still
plot her abduction from fertile mythos
in inexact replication of every situation.
"Beautiful back, beautiful, sinuous, grace-driven back,
with only primitive political ideas,
a great curved organ for paradox, called 'spine',
I'm going to caress you with my breath, in time with your fifth
unliterary sense, with my rainbow brush!"
I would not mind being leaned against your back and shot!
Viva To All That!
Believe me, I would. The fields are real, they are knowable, they
exist, there is nothing bigger than them,
not even our two human bosses: Mister Time & Comrade Timing.
It is not as a poet I speak but as a pedestrian & a boy.
People, love your waitresses and your bus drivers,
& the veins that run from the back of the bus
where the crazies retch,
to the front where the depressed
think everything is their fault,
& the paranoiacs
that nothing is.
Oh, sad is their song!

Outings

Y Un Canción Por E.

We are elements of design just now.
We can't decide between food or love.
This is such thick book I fear
it will take years to read.
Don't got it. Fresh out.
A week? Don't got that neither.
A day? A night? Too long.
An hour then? A minute?
OK, but you must hurry.
Close the book. Let's
Run. Jump over the fat Turk
scarfing up the van.
Put your face in mine,
roll up your skin in mine,
save space as well as time,
don't get tangled
in the tugboat lines,
they're there for other crimes.
Cut across fields,
streak through alleys, go
over the national defenses
of several small
nations. Like that.
And you who hold the soap bubble
between your chopsticks
over us like an umbrella
over two sick mammals
see that what quivers under
is merely animation
to throw into relief
what rages above,
cheek, eyes, lips, etc. Oh love.
Has watching hit a snag,
is everybody's watch
broke or in decline?

Quite fine thank you,
having a life.
I didn't say intriguing,
I said weird. And all.

Christmas In New York

for Laura

Trees torpedoes Soviet galoshes
books violins woolen socks
Mexico Argentina Korea Peru.
We promenade in steamy human corn.
An actress with her arm wrapped
around gift-wrapped mannequin
calls mom in snowbound Arkansas.
People people the island
wrapped around each other
lit scroll-like Chinese on
Chinatown marquee
where we suck duck feet
that once walked the sturdy earth.
Oh tender feet whose flesh we sweetly suck!
The string on our hearts is nigh undone.
Ghosts nine feet tall come bounding through the slush!
We are so nicely dressed!
Parcels with wings in ghostly disarray
argue with their lost souls in traffic
gifts exchanged desperately fast!
We tangle ourselves to wind-whipped
humanity blowing about the future
when our children will have nice toys.
The world has a million elbows
resting on fine tables in the bistro de la vida.
All exchange is slush balderdash
o great haberdasher!
O pure metal money.
O truth under duress – this being
that time – there are no words
that are not for sale. Yet we know:
outside the body begins the lie.
Outside that the newspaper.

And the bum wrapped in it
will not change tomorrow's news
though tomorrow both paper and body
will be a white mound of snow,
an unsystematic library, confusion
of what lived and what died
before it could be re-read
or how from inside ourselves
the big snow came
to invade with beauty
so recently rent a world.
The magic lounges wrapped
in jukebox steam
give good detail to whatever makes it in.
O baby, call in the the surface-to-air messenger,
the caffeinated pigeon
with the beating of his trained
telegraph across the *années.*
O differentiated lumps of *amore!*
O garbage dump masses having us for dinner
you on a platter me on a cloud!
Food for everybody.
L'âme de Madame is now served.
Erectile tissue paper in crêpe de chine
rose-pinks to burst its mauve bows.
Death to the military metaphors:
sentences, captains, bullets, reports.
Without a roof we revel in being,
wrapped for others – keepsakes
of a state and time when
human beings are:

1) rubber animals who bend well and far
   held tightly between frozen mitts

2) empty drawing on swirling imagoes to make credible thickness
   i.e., belabored snowmen and snowwomen

3) impressions on Japanese screen

4) comic algebra

5) excess food covered by tweed

6) mute newlyweds wrapped in a single fur

7) baby mimes doing stuff with their toes

8) company representatives (the Trans-
    Siberian Railroad, the Alaska goldrush)

9) travel dust from luminous hair
    of aliens with cuneiform legs
dancing the poignant resiliency of almost anything

10) hardy gossamer.

The juke pivots in the end-century
for Genghis wherever he is,
and Elvis Kahn, tailor to history,
in Jersey over the smoke where he
cuts the falling snow to fit
everyone so they'll look sublime:
newts en masque, popes en croûte,
flares on restaurant tables
where the dons of beauty &
donnas of grace pose
in the unfathomable
instrumentation of seated self.
The Dream of Perfection neatly fits
the Dream of Wickedness about the waist
of the Dream of Power 'round the testes
of the Dream of Transformation.
Above the wingèd tedium
of phones ringing in Christmas splendor
the party calls us to the source

of the objective world
whose diamond opens briefly
like a disco at some pink odd point
where commerce ceases and exchange begins
& dreaming well accoutred
in pleasure and so dry.

A Leafy Angel

to the Columns Hotel

Quietly at the corner table
where the dry fountain
drowns in unswept leaves
under its disconsolate angel,
the slim boy in the shadow
of the blooming jeune fille
has opened Postmodern Art,
a book. Twixt happiness
and unhappiness
the only break we get
she thinks is sleep.
Certain mental interiors
exist only in French
is what he thinks.
Stranger still she is chief thespian
in a play
taking place presently in her mind
where she does bad things
in order to build capital
for masturbation
with a visiting European
on whose shoulders
run little trains
powered by oblivion.
At the streetcar stop
an old woman in mourning black
watches her younger self run
alongside a mostly naked runner
following the streetcar line
to a perfect body.
They are Jasmine and Sweet Olive,
they have just met
in 1924 in The City

That Lives for Its Belles,
a bar.
Stranger, sit quietly here
this evening
at the Columns Hotel
on the terrace at dusk
where light goes out with flair
on froufrou and history.
Outside the body, happily,
begins the lie.

Outings

1.

Happiness reaches for the contract that will end it – and an ass like a broasted chicken. Hawk-eyed from the leatherette he saw the undoneness of it, the edge-of-litter scallopishness – it's where interest roots & digs and would rather read, he explained to someone so unaccustomed to her surroundings that he was engulfed by the sentiment that there is no boredom in the presence of genuine difference. The joy of knowing that complex carbohydrates can be had later doubled his giddiness and soon they were sailing to where he would do her how the French do vegetables – grill tomatoes, grate carrots, pour oil & wine on eggplant, let them lie around for a week until they become formaldehyde – but of course he would not because that would detract from the cherries and framboises of which such an evening was constructed, and he would certainly not take her to the place where particulars surrender their uniqueness to Mr. Cliché. When all is said and done a night out is the only escape from people who kill in their sleep in the name of snap beans and spinach. And nothing is said and done until one is far out of the way where the public exchange is frivolous and violent, ineffective and free – which is right here, where I hang out.

2.

There is so little interest in prose where he comes from it's a lingo nobody grokks. You've lost your ear long before you finished your sentence. Alone you mumble yourself back into poetry. It's your sentence to finish. And yet there are stories, like carrots, pushing through topsoil all red and horny like dicks awakened by an Old Story. To grate them and chop 'em like the French do is no great feat but to wave them about like scepters and to point things on the map with them, ah, that is Pedagogy! And there are times, darling. No vegetable amour lasts, hélas! One can trust a carrot to rot. Red hair and all. Our amours based on the denial of decay (those decrepit trovadores) is indecent. Tomatoes I have no truck with, they are poison, the very idea of them! Societal ideas of beauty, modified nightshade! To achieve extreme red and go via Peter Max to the trough of the color-blind! Well, it's a living, but your grandmother snickers. And you eggplant, the last vegetable on earth, have transcended obscenity in your chosen purpleness that no oil – which you absorb like a child absorbs television – or wine will ever an iota diminish. Queen of veggies, love of my loins, there is enough tragedy in your shape and my ludicrousness to keep the decayed trovadores in layers for years. I seek my fate among the vegetables because I owe them an apology! I owe cherries and stromberries nuttin! With champagne they went down on the silk beds and the undecayable humans on them were overcome and taken by waves of giddy chatter! They are the core & body of the book that is about them, clean like Roman, elegant like Palatino, complex like Gothic. The hand lingers and is pleased, the rag content is high and even, one can make clothes from this book, wear them over an aroused nakedness to the edge of the pit where the damned roll with the veggies in hot oil. And be comforted & above & care not a damn! It's these Christian specks in the binding that are the trouble: they bugle to their counterparts in the grainy film for playback, regression, slo-mo & compassion. Hundreds of years ago I was a slave trader in Alexandria. It was there that I first met my blond barbarian wife for whose love I converted to the new fad & died in the catacombs, slaveless and sorry. Taste the whip that drives the lightning! Never one to give up anything, whether a woman or an idea, I yield both whip and censer and not on myself that often either! And they interest me, vegetables, for those domestic interludes, those infinite Sundays stretched like Maria Callas's voice between the perils of the diurnal. There you have it. Nobody sets up hierarchies and heraldries better than us, it is what we practice in the relentless cornucopia. And no one sets up deeper and crueler ones than the hopefully indifferent. Which may be only careful inattention and a slow, slow dying like a brilliant sun in the pipes of a Pan flute on a mountain. Plenitude is available but it will cost you nothing, and there are things between you and I that will not allow us to get away without paying.

3.

Much as it tries to recall the nurse, the mind cares only about language. She is reading a book on the steps below you and smoking a very good, very long cigarette. Self-satisfied smoke ascends to the skies with the message: "Elmore Leonard is good." The atmosphere has quickened since she has crossed her legs at your kitchen table. She is no longer reading a book, and her cigarette smoke ascends barely to the top of the refrigerator where it sits, saying nothing. The peace on the stairs has become the tense string of a crossbow aimed at the genital deer who is already, alas, lying quite still on the rug between you. Not a wild deer exactly but it came cheap from the zoo. The hard plastic yellow chair. The Summer dance program has barely started and already she is not free. A physical therapist who brings the dead back via vigor and vim, she asks herself why. Wouldn't they be better off free? Turning the genital deer loose, letting the dying go, putting down the crossbow. Dance, dance, that's where dance comes, giving notice to taut strings, tame deer, the painfully dying, that there are other motions, wilder beasts, better ways to meet your maker the molecule shaker. But there is talk, small, razor-sharp talk, trimming hedges, checking information, probing memory – big words, little words, looking for the places between motions, the ingress of wilder beasts, the egress of souls, to there plant themselves, spiders of reason, to quickly weave supports, bridges, levees. What can Elmore Leonard and smoke do about it? My shoulder muscles hurt terribly. Down there? Yes, down there, down there very far where the already slain steak awaits its master the cook, that deformed being laden with eggplants. You are naked – no book, no smoke – on your back. Above you is the terrible nurse of the sky, all sharp points of light appealing sweetly to something simple. Do you have any oil? A long cotton skirt, a cloud, floats under the stars. It is hanging by the hook of a question: do you have any oil? God in his wisdom made oil. He made oil so that the gears of this sometimes dry planet would shift smoothly and there will be no terrible creak of the axis mundi. She is very tall, as befits the cosmic axis, and from her motion, her slow rotation, oil is made, and it flows. No longer domestic, the dead deer rises from the stew and is reconstituted in a wilder beast. The soul may exit now, it does not care to stay here. It stands above your neck and shoulders where her hands are and is asking its own slowly important questions: If there is center will it do to wait until it is reached? If the center is everywhere wouldn't the sooner be the better? On your back and above your buttocks the questions become more insistent, the soul is in a veritable froth of philosophy. And at long last she arrives, first at the center of you, then at the center of herself. There is recognition, surprise . . . a human. Not a deer after all. An axial encounter, suspension, nice to meet you. She kneads your buttocks, slaps them down on the floured board and weaves a bread from it & it bakes alone under her breath. We eat this bread at weddings & funerals, strictly ritual, comprendé? The firmness that now enters the world resembles nothing current but its authority . . . olé! If stairs hatch in the shadow of a caress the real city grows in real caressing . . . no more smoke. Civilization has a job to do. On the inside of your thighs pushed open by her thighs there is great purpose . . . builders with blueprints, engineers in mudboots, architects with 104° fever. There is an axis to erect, an axis mundi, more oil, the purpose is at last plain, who's got time for books? But there are the calves. And the ankles. And the feet. The feet that have taken you here and her here and that are going to take you and her away in different directions come completion of the project, after the burgers move in. They are full of nerve endings and their own cooperative sensitivity and a sense of purpose next to which the sexual act pales, is but ersatz religion. The feet they trod. In the sun of the empire that your sex built they will march. In the moon of the pastoral rug your sentiment has on black velvet woven they will dance and run and leap and then run away, dance into the dark, leap onto a tree. They are in fact so alive and strong that you forget your erection, and it disappears. The sky disconnects, the earth is loosened from its moorings, space drifts into its component dimensions. Call for the hands! There is an urgent call for the hands! Hands, you are wanted in every room! All at once the inhabitants of the beautiful city have become patients, their dwellings sick rooms. Conjure the hands, and they arrive, fully fleshed and as sure of their job as the feet. They are on your face, kneading your cheeks, other breads, etc, and your eyes, pulsing inward, recovering a fleeting . . . deer. Big drops of hot salty sweat fall from one forehead onto another, scorching the imaginary loci of agony. A drop lands in your mouth, it is the taste of what it means, your tongue savors it, that's where cooking begins to take on life. Mmmmm, that's mmmm to you, peasants. Darting tongue, hummingbird, the sick will get well. And your erection, the one you hold in common between you, begins its steady climb back into the recessed heavens, the shrunken hells, filling them up, baking them, they all rise and are firm once more. Ah, ancient world here we are! She rounds your hips, a butte with a wheel turning to draw oil, each spoke spoken once, a long time ago, the meaning clear, the words forgotten. What was the shadow of a caress is now another kind of pressure, an itch to scribble almost. To cover the page Keats had such longing for with those dances of ink, gold and purple, whence eggplants draw their happy shapes. Itch that mounts in her palms as they look to come together for prayer with the thin and thinner and finally transparent sheet of your body between them. A rosary or a pebble, worn smooth by the itching palms meaning to meet with the world between them. Thighs open apart and up, and then the effort is realized but not in the hopeful way. Something has to be said, she realizes, and she does. That's not part of it, she says. I know, you say, but I can't help it. Sweat drops land on your stomach and one directly on the tip of your penis now pointing to all that can't be said. It smarts, that's where they are. You are afraid of your feet, remembering them from the other side, from before, when the armies had the sun in front of them and massaged the soldiers' nodes with alacrity and cruelty. Pray for your erection against feet and language, friends, and you will save yourself. There is only the gaze left, your last ally, and you do, you look, she at it, you at her and it, she at you and it, and there are such rugged scapes, carved by language everywhere, words trudging up slopes, wrinkles rolled hot crêpe-like around phrases and admonitions. And they come, surely enough, up to the gaze like fireflies, moths, skitters, succubi and suckabooms. The unhidden caress is unprotected and raw and full of overt honey, flowing oil and outside-pointing sides and inward roundness exposed. She looks and is distractedly kneading, and the bread feels and falls flat. Who's gonna feed the fucking masses,

I ask you, if all these words have their way? Under her skirt, where her buttocks are, your hands are trapped of their own will in the damp prison of silk. Your lean head is below her belly, at the junction where all these trains are heading, full of Nazis, tourists, prisoners, cattle, loot. It could be any war, but it's this one. It is hot here. No, she says, we must telegraph someone to come, to blow up sections of the track, what we are making is just another civilization. Kissed hot the triangle of her pubis luxuriates under silk and cotton putting forth both the oils and the beings they are attempting to choreograph. Lie back down, my soul, obey my hands and my face and her friendly body, lie back, fully erect, and we promise you the recognition you crave and for which you went so deep into those trovadores. She stands there and I stand there. Who knows what suspended time is sharpening a full set of steak knives outside the admittedly infinite room? What should I do with you? she says, I take you in my mouth. There is a place there where words used to be and nothing in the warm cave remembers their being. Their furniture has vanished as if they never lived there, no lithos on the wall, no hairpins, no mementoes. The cave is original and will have it that words never lived there. Escaped from her lips like a swarm leaving behind only a cloud of forgetfulness, they have taken off for the unwritten books, the potential libraries. These are the parted lips wrapped in their fullness about the hard-on it has taken such effort to write. And would they speak, my lips, fastened below on her nether, as they say, lips, have they locked the word between them? As above as below, and if the words have escaped so be it. And if they have not, they are jailed and will not leave and will have to become the flesh they torture. What were they, these words? Questions, they were always questions, all these words were nothing but questions hidden under affirmative masks, fashioned out of absence and disjointness. And the watching, that is only the delighted warden making sure that the fastening lasts, that the words will not escape with the sigh that is sure to come. It would be good now to assign this watching to an other, an indifferent other, and God is born this way, an assignment in the face of inevitable consummation. Please. Artfully, He is born from this assignment, as indifferent as we need to make Him. But what will He do when we part? He will

Speak. Yes, He will Speak, and He will make us speak too, make us speak for Him, assign speech to us because we have assigned indifference to Him. Please, we say, she to me and I to her. Please do not let us come to that place where we'll have to free our warden from his job. Please, keep us from the assignment we will surely have to fulfill, please, please, please. This is prayer, born in the knowledge of imminent orgasm, inevitable consummation. Are you sure, my mouth asks her mouth, are you sure, her mouth asks my erection. Are you sure, are you sure? Should we free God, should we? We quicken and are bountifully imploded. Mmmmm, mmmmm, that's mmmmm, mmmmm, to you, peasants. There is the shuddering and the tightening to make sure that nothing escapes, and there are people outside, knocking at the door, wanting in. Our guests have arrived. There is an open book on the table, and speaking smoke and a dead deer. Puleeze! Next time, God don't take no chances.

Acknowledgements

"The Other End" appeared in *Sulfur 16* (1986, Los Angeles).

"Mnemogasoline" appeared in *New Directions Annual 51* (1987, New York) and in a special section of *Stiletto One*, with illustrations by James Dean Pruner (1989, Lawrence, Kansas, Michael Annis, editor). A section of "Mnemogasoline," entitled "What to Do About Art," appeared in the programme of the 8th Annual Taos Poetry Circus (June 1989, Taos, New Mexico) in connection with the World Heavyweight Poetry Championship, a bardic event that takes place at the Summer Solstice every year in Taos, Peter Rabbit and Annie McNaughton, organizers. I was Heavyweight Poetry Champion in 1987, after defeating two-time champ Lewis MacAdams. I was, in my turn, beaten by Victor Hernandez Cruz in 1988, who defended his title well against Deborah Salazar, but was deposed by Anne Waldman in 1989. The following year, Waldman defended her crown against Ed Sanders, and in 1991 challenges Ntozake Shange.

"Telyric" was in *Open 24 Hours* (1986, Baltimore, Chris Toll, editor). The poem was written in connection with a documentary on baseball, *Boys With Bats* (Deanna Kamiel, director, KTCA-TV Minneapolis). The baseball reference is to the interview I conducted with the Nicaraguan pitcher, Dennis Martinez.

"Roto: How The Bourgeoisie Dreams" was published in *Tone* (Spring 1986, S. R. Rage Gallery, New York).

"Y Un Canción Por E." and "The Introduction" were published in different versions in *Sideshow Magazine One* (1989, Pontiac, Michigan, Nancy A. Brosky and Glen Armstrong, editors).

"Circle Jerk" was published in *Chelsea 47* (1988, New York). A slightly different version appeared in the premiere issue of *Avec* (1988, San Francisco).

"Casino Pierre" was published in *Talisman: A Journal of Contemporary Poetry & Poetics* (1988, Hoboken, New Jersey).

"Virgin Mule" appeared in *Bombay Gin* (1988, Boulder, Colorado), and in Romanian translation in *Agora 2* (1988, Washington, DC, Dorin Tudoran, editor).

"Seeing Out Of The Sub" was a broadside published on the occasion of a poetry reading at Cody's Bookstore (1986, Berkeley, California). It was also published in *The Southwestern Review*, Spring 1989.

"Demands Of Exile" was published in the *Black Buzzard Review* (1988, Maine).

"Christmas In New York" was in *Fine Madness*, Volume Six, Number 2 (Seattle, Washington, Fall-Winter 1989/90).

"Leaves of Nerves" was published in a limited edition by Minnesota Center for Book Arts and printed by Coffee House Press for Walker Art Center.